THE TRUTH OF YOUR REALITY

Insights on the game of life and how you choose to play it

BY NEREEDA MCINNES

Copyright © 2017 by Nereeda McInnes.
All rights reserved. This book or any portion thereof may not be reproduced or used in any manner whatsoever without the express written permission of the publisher except for the use of brief quotations in a book review.

Publishing Services provided by Paper Raven Books
Printed in the United States of America and Australia
First Printing, 2017

Ebook 978-0-6480541-0-8
Paperback 978-0-6480541-1-5
Hardback 978-0-6480541-2-2

If life is but a game... how will you play?

TABLE OF CONTENTS

	Introduction	1
1.	The Game	11
2.	What Is Reality?	21
3.	What Are You Wearing?	31
4.	Heads Or Tails	41
5.	What You See Is What You Get	49
6.	Know Better, Do Better?	57
7.	Good Vibrations	63
8.	The Relationship Factor	73
9.	Are You Willing To Explore?	83
10.	Game On	93
	Afterword	97
	Acknowledgments	99
	Resources	101
	About The Author	105
	More From The Author	107

INTRODUCTION

This book is based on what I believe to be true. My reality. The reality that works for me.

Before you dive into the book, it is important for me to say that everything you read within these pages is based on the truth of my reality, at the time of writing. I am by no means here to tell you what to think. If anything, my intention is simply to ask you to ponder your own reality and what makes sense for you. I even understand that once this book goes to print, I may well indeed change my view on how my personal reality works. However, as it stands, the questions I have and the insights I share are simply that. Any references or research materials I refer to can be found at the back of this book, under the resources section. At the end of each chapter, you will find a "Check Point". This is a summary of the questions posed within each chapter for you to review, should you wish to explore further. This is completely up to you of course!

Like anything, if there are some parts of the book that don't resonate with you, don't discount the entire thing. There's no point writing off the entire smorgasbord simply because you didn't like the prawns!

The Reality That Works for You

I have been blessed to know and be surrounded by many awesome people, and a few that have been not so awesome (you know the ones in your life). Each person, though, has been just as important to the story of my life as the other.

One dear friend of mine, though almost ten years younger, shared much in common with me when it came to our outlook on life. She would call me a mentor sometimes, which was humbling. But I learned as much about myself from her as she did from me.

We shared many in-depth chats about life, the way things were for us, and how they might be for others. Each with an open mind, we explored and spoke of the possibilities in our world and for our lives.

One particular day, we were chatting about her beautiful parents, two people of whom she adores. She spoke of how they always watched the news and all the current affairs programs. Although they enjoyed doing this together, at times it left them feeling depressed, as all they ever seemed to see were the bad things going on in the world.

My friend was upset that they felt like this and wanted them to see things another way. But she knew this was how they liked to live—it was what they had always done, after all.

INTRODUCTION

It was in that moment, I said that they were simply *"living in a reality that worked for them"*. And although it wasn't a reality that worked for my friend, neither was right nor wrong, it just was.

When those eight words came out of my mouth, I never forgot them. It was like someone else had said it, allowing me to share in the epiphany. It made so much sense, because we *all* do it. We all live in the reality that works for us. The reality that is true for us.

Perhaps then, when reading this book and deciding which parts resonate with you and which parts don't, keep in mind this fantastic quote by the lovely Anita Moorjani: "I'm not asking you to believe in me, I'm asking you to believe in yourself."

I believe we are all very powerful, magnificent creatures who, while living in the truth of our own reality at any given time, can do so many amazing things, if only we believed it.

I also believe that you have the power to do whatever it is you are called to do. If you don't know what that is just yet, please don't worry. Don't compare yourself to those who do. Instead, embrace the exploration. Embrace the experience of simply being human; a person who, at this very moment, stands exactly where you are, an absolute miracle.

The fact that you are here right now, in this moment in time, is no mistake. You are a gift. You, my friend, are you and the universe all rolled into one. A powerful speck of brilliance already perfect just the way you are. Whether you feel that way now or not, know this—you matter. And I am so grateful you are here.

The Coat

When I was growing up, I created a group called "The Explorers", which I semi-forced both of my sisters to join. In my mind, and in the backyard of our house in the western suburbs of South Australia, I would imagine big rocks, caves and creeks we could explore. I even wanted to get Explorers t-shirts made.

I loved to see what was out there. I always imagined how cool it would be if everyone I knew lived in the same street and the roads were made of water instead of cement. We could row our boats to each other's houses and go exploring anytime we liked!

I have always been an explorer and someone who questions things, a mini philosopher you might say. I have no doubt this is why I love to question things and the status quo of life to this day.

As I have gotten older, done much deep and sometimes very painful personal work, peeled layers off the onion of me, so to speak, and come to where I am, my self-awareness has grown. I can see all that is and all that was, through a brand-new lens.

INTRODUCTION

I can see that throughout my life, I had been living in a reality that was true for me. In fact, this reality has always been true, no matter what stage I have been at. And this is the same for you, too. My thoughts, my beliefs, all that was and now is, has been a total reflection of everything I know to be true. Then and now.

What I didn't know growing up, was that I had a choice about what to believe. For most of us, when we are young, this is generally the case. It is our parents and those we are surrounded by most who have been our greatest influence. We didn't know any different then and as the new-to-the-world sponges that we were, we soaked up every word, felt every feeling and learned to be who we are. It is only with the benefit of hindsight, self-awareness, forgiveness and understanding that we now see things for what they were or might have been.

We later discover, too, that our parents didn't know everything and were just doing the best they knew how. We learn that the people who hurt us in our lives were also hurt themselves. We learn that some people appeared to be just plain evil and that others had the biggest hearts you had ever come across.

The whole way though, throughout it all, we created a persona for ourselves based on who we thought we were and what others thought we should be. We rebelled, we misunderstood and we fought against things without even knowing why. And if we were lucky, we kept going and kept learning. All the while, adding on a layer of belief about ourselves and the world, each step of the way.

Until later, when we start to realise those layers feel more like a giant coat—and that giant coat of ingrained beliefs and perceptions we have been wearing, may actually be weighing us down, inhibiting us from moving freely in the direction of who we really are, simply because it is too darn heavy.

It is then we realise we need to loosen up the coat. That, in fact, we need to learn how to *un-learn*.

We also realise that loosening up that coat isn't going to take five minutes. In fact, it may well be a life-long exercise, with some of the hardest parts either showing themselves at the start, popping up when we least expect it, or when we are ready to see. It's all part of our coat, nonetheless.

With this realisation, we start to get a sense of just how uncomfortable our coat is—and perhaps how painful it may be to start removing the layers. Because, when we take off one layer, not only will we need to see, accept and heal what is there, we may also find more underneath. More for us to work on, more for us to realise, more for us to explore.

It is at that point, many people decide to keep the coat on and leave things buried. To tuck their painful memories in a jacket pocket or in their singlets, right underneath so no one will ever see. The thing is though, whether people can see it or not, it is still there, part of you. And until you look at that thing, take it out, and see it for what it is, you are not able to heal. It will remain there, a part of you until you are ready to deal with it, or until it is ready to make itself known in other ways.

We have our own dirt, painful memories, shame, sadness, loss, anger, guilt and frustration sitting there under our coats, waiting to be cleaned, to be healed. But until we are ready, until we are aware, or until we choose to remember, there it will remain. And we will simply continue to live in the reality that is working, or not working, for us.

Our body, a miraculous thing, will whisper when it has something to heal. If you don't heed the whisper, it will start talking louder. If you ignore that, it will get even louder still. Eventually, if you do nothing, it will smack you over the head with a serious diagnosis or something else significant to get your attention.

Some of us need that smack in the face, while some of us will heed the whisper. Either way, the journey and the reality will be true for you. Why? Because you create your own reality. What you believe to be true always will be, until you experience something that tells you different.

Perception Is Reality

We all know the law of cause and effect, that what you put out, you get back. It's a simple concept to understand, yet we often feel powerless. The thing is, we are the power. We are the centre of our own universe, whilst being part of the entire universe. We are one and the same. You are me, and I am you. We are made up of energy that can heal, empower and change the world.

But we don't believe we can. Why? Because of everything we have learned, the challenges we have faced and the perception we have of who we are.

I'm sure you have heard the saying, "perception is reality". And how true this is. I used to run around 10-15 minutes late for work a lot. Those who worked by the clock looked down upon my ways and complained. What they didn't see was that I would work until 10-11 pm many a night. They only saw when I arrived to work. Their perception was that I was lazy and didn't respect start times. And I can certainly see why they would think this. But I knew I was working extremely hard. Still, it didn't matter. Their view was their view, and it wasn't up to me to change it. Their perception was their reality and therefore true for them.

I am not here to tell you how to live—it is your reality after all. If you believe in synchronicity, if that is indeed your reality, then you will know you aren't reading this book by chance. You are holding this in your hands right now because somewhere along the way, you wanted to remember. You wanted that reminder that you are one hell of a miracle. That you are here to be all that you can be and to remember who you are—and that is magnificent, in every sense of the word.

With that in mind, my wish for you, wherever this may meet you, is to find the truth of your reality and create a life that allows you the freedom to be all you can be. So, pop on your Explorers' t-shirt and let's dive in together.

Or, as Graham Norton likes to say, "Let's get on with the show!"

Chapter 1

THE GAME

If life is but a game, then how you choose to play it is completely up to you. Notice I say "if". Because, whilst I can tap into my own intuition and know what makes sense for me, it may not feel the same for you. You may feel it is nothing of the sort. So then, who is right and who is wrong? Well, we are both right. Why? Because we are both operating out of our own reality—a reality that works for us. Or doesn't, depending on what is going on in our lives.

For me, I see life as a bit of a game. Each and every one of us is the main player of the game of life we have chosen for ourselves. We are the artist and the brush. We are the driver in the driver's seat. We are the master of our own destiny. In each moment, we create our own reality and we make choices. Sometimes with conscious thought and other times not. Either way, we are still the main player.

When it comes to understanding why we are here, what our purpose is and what we are supposed to do with our time on this planet, it can sometimes seem so complicated and overwhelming that some of us prefer to not think about it at all. I don't think we need to make it that hard though. There is enough complication out there if we wish to seek it out.

By seeing life as a game that you choose how to play, knowing that you will be faced with different challenges and opportunities to grow along the way—that you get to choose the players you want on your team, and to learn from those you wish weren't, understanding they are there to either teach or learn from you—makes life an exciting, exhilarating and amazing opportunity to create the ultimate, always-evolving masterpiece of *you*.

There are some significant facts in this lil' ol' game of ours. Each of us, every living thing and even things that are not, are made up of energy. Each of which, vibrating at many a frequency, but vibrating just the same. This energy is something that we all share.

What does this mean? It means that we are not separate from anything. We are, in fact, all connected. Every decision we make, everything we feel and all that we are is intertwined. Who we are affects not only ourselves and each other, but the entire universe.

I know that sounds big, and so it should! You are a magnificent miracle, playing the game of life on this glorious planet we call Earth. And whilst you may be a speck of sand or drop in the ocean when it comes to the relative size of who you are in this moment, your importance and magnificence is the size of the entire universe.

Whoa! Pretty huge, right? So how is it that you got to play this game of life anyway? How did you get here, and what are you supposed to do while you are here?

We Are All Connected

I have done much personal development and research through reading, watching interviews, listening to podcasts and discerning what different experts say in many different fields, including life, reality, ancient traditions, spirituality, metaphysics, the universe and more. What I found, with science having proven that we are made up of energy and that we are indeed all connected, is that it stands to reason we all share one consciousness.

This has been described as many different things. Gregg Braden calls it The Divine Matrix. Anita Moorjani calls it the great tapestry of life. In Chinese medicine, it is referred to as Chi. Hindu tradition refers to it as Prana. Then, there's God force, higher self, Holy Spirit, Ki and in the movie *Star Wars*, they call it The Force.

There's no denying that this consciousness exists. Perhaps we have not seen it directly with our own eyes, but of course that doesn't mean it's not there. We don't need to see love to feel it. Just like we can't see the cool breeze of the wind on our face; we just know it exists.

Therefore, not only are we connected, we are everyone that ever was or is. Perhaps different variations of each, but connected just the same. With that in mind, anyone you ever meet, anyone you ever judge, anyone you are ever critical of, anyone you ever hold in high esteem, anyone you have any feeling or emotion towards, is part of you. They are with you, simply sharing time on this planet, this human experience, at the same time. All the while, each soul here to learn what it is they came here for.

That Is Real Which Never Changes

I'll never forget the way Dr. Wayne Dyer explained the soul, the essence of who we are, in a talk at the Wanderlust Conference in 2012, titled, "The Art of Manifesting".* I wasn't at the talk in person, I watched it through the power of YouTube (how great it is that we can learn and connect this way). Wayne spoke of his mother, who had passed away just two days before at the time of his talk. Many of us would not be able to stand and talk about our loved one having just passed, yet for Wayne, with his knowledge, outlook and understanding of life and all that is, he could do this with both love and ease.

He began by speaking about what his teacher and guru in India said when asked the question, "What is real?" To this, his teacher answered, "That is real which never changes, everything else is illusion."

THE GAME

Wayne spoke of the photos of his mother he had hanging on the walls in his apartment in Maui. In one picture, it is 1926 and his mother is 10 years old. In another, she is reading a poem two years later at the age of 12. He then spoke about the many other pictures he had of her, some when she was 30, and one when she was sitting on his lap for her 75th birthday.

He then asked, "So, which one is my mother?" She is older in some and young in others. As his teacher had said, that is real which never changes. "So, what is it that makes up my mother?" he asked.

He went on to say that when he was 21 years old, he believed that his body was who he was, and he was certain that it was real. He then joked, saying that he has been searching for his 21-year-old body for years, but just can't seem to find it anywhere!

True to this, Wayne's mother was never the same in any picture. She was always changing and growing, but her essence, her soul, the spirit and light in which she is, that never changed. Only you can't see that, you just know that it's her.

Wayne went on to explain this another way. If you had weighed his mother one second before she died and one second after she died, she would have weighed exactly the same—yet she was no longer alive. So her life, our life, is actually weightless, formless. It has no beginning, it has no end. It is infinite. This analogy helps to explain that we are not our body, that we are, in fact, a spiritual being having a human experience.

Why Are We Here?

Why then have so many of us chosen what seem to be incredibly challenging lives filled with much suffering and pain? My understanding, along with others, is that before we choose to come into this world, we decide what it is we must learn in our next lifetime—that which is for the highest benefit of our soul's evolution. Why else would there be so many people in poverty in one place and affluence aplenty in another?

Each person on this planet, you and I, made the choice to come through at the exact time we did, to ensure we were in the best possible position to learn what is most important for us to learn in this life time. That isn't to say that everything is set in stone for the evolution of you. It simply means that you will be faced with challenges, or better yet, opportunities, to grow along the way so you can evolve.

It is in these moments and experiences you get to choose how you will play the game. Will you choose to be the victim? Will you choose to overcome adversity? Will you see the beauty in the pain? Will you see only pain? The choice is yours, because anything that happens in this game of life is neither right, wrong, good or bad. We ourselves are the ones who put meaning to it.

That doesn't change or lessen the pain and suffering, nor does it take away the joy and rapture we experience in our lives. It just means, the meaning you give to it is up to you. Some things may be too painful and require time for grieving before a decision can be made about what that experience has provided you. And how you feel about something may indeed change over time, too. Ultimately though, it is you who chooses what each experience means for you, in your reality. After all, who is anyone else to tell you how to feel and how you should react?

Cause and Effect

This leads me to the next part of how awesome you are. Just as everything else is made up of energy, so too are your thoughts, feelings, emotions, beliefs and actions. Your thoughts lead to feelings and your feelings to thoughts. It's like when you hear a certain song on the radio, or visit a certain place from your childhood, which stirs up a feeling that then generates a thought memory, emotion, or both.

Your beliefs will determine what is possible for you or anyone else, at any given moment in time. As Henry Ford famously said, "Whether you think you can or think you can't, you are right." Your emotions create positive or negative thoughts and actions in the same way.

This is where the law of cause and effect, or law of attraction, comes into play, which states that for every effect there is a definite cause, and likewise for every cause, there is a definite effect. Your thoughts, behaviours and actions create specific effects. In other words, like attracts like. All of which creates your personal experience, your reality.

Depending on how we have been playing the game of our life so far, we may feel powerless and not in control of our lives. We may see things as happening to us rather than for us. We may be experiencing turmoil, or we may have spent many years meditating each day, experiencing a connection to all that is, in a most profound way. Or not.

Whatever the case, everything up until this point has been there for us to learn, grow and remember the magnificence of who we are. Why else would we be here, if not for that? And with that incredible understanding, the more we choose to understand ourselves, grow and shed our skin, the more self-aware we become, the more compassionate we become and the more we begin to see who we are, as well as the beauty in all that is and all that we are a part of.

With this outlook, with the knowledge that we are all connected, that our thoughts, feelings, beliefs and actions create our reality, that our world does indeed abide by the law of cause and effect, and with the understanding that we are all exactly where we need to be in terms of the evolution of our soul's journey, and the lessons we seek—perhaps the only question that then remains is, how will you choose to play the game?

Check Point

- If you took a step back and looked at your life as if you were watching it on a television, what would you see?

- Who is supporting you in the movie of your life? What would you change? What are you grateful for?

Chapter 2

WHAT IS REALITY?

A little while ago, I learned that there are over 4,000 religions in the world. Everyone who subscribes to each religion believes theirs is the right one. And that is true for each of them, because it is their reality. They may not have always believed in this religion, or maybe they have been following it their whole lives. Perhaps they will change and decide to follow another course of action. Who knows? It doesn't matter. Their religion, dogma, and spiritual or atheist beliefs are theirs. It is their reality. They have created it and they get to choose what to do with it.

So then, if everyone creates their own reality, shouldn't we accept it? We may not choose to live it or even agree with it, and that is our choice. Just as we may choose to help those less fortunate than us, or choose to follow a spiritual path over a religious one. Again, it's our choice.

Your Reality

Your reality is what you make it. It is as real and true for you as anything that is fact. To others, though, it is subjective. Why? Because they are viewing your reality through the eyes of their own reality. You may agree with a shared perspective or agree to disagree. Both of these choices would be deemed "right" in the reality of each person.

The truth of your reality always lies within you. Asking yourself questions about it is one of the best ways to understand yourself and who you really are at a deeper level.

What is your reality, then? What are you creating with that magnificent self of yours? What are you believing? Who are the people in your life? What are they teaching you? How are you reacting to the events that occur around you? Are you stuck? Are you growing? Are some parts awesome while others seemingly the opposite?

As you pause to think about this, consider these questions: what are you accepting and what are you allowing? If we are here to learn and grow, what are the situations in your life trying to teach you? Do you get angry at certain people or events taking place in the world? If so, what can you do about it? Does it stir up something in you that perhaps needs to be addressed or healed, does it inspire you to help and make a difference—or perhaps both?

When you choose to explore who you are, what works for you, and what is no longer serving you, it's important to take stock of where you are right now. Asking these questions can help you do that. It requires you to be completely honest with yourself about all aspects of you, to see things without judgement and to accept all that is in this present moment.

Acceptance

Acceptance is one of the most empowering things you can do for yourself. No matter what you have gone through, accepting where you are now is key. It allows you to acknowledge all that you are, and what you have learned up until this point. With acceptance, whatever it looks like to you, you can step forward into the next moments of your life with a clean slate. You can attract that which you desire, by creating and embodying new thoughts, feelings, beliefs and emotions for yourself—to start creating a life that feels good for you.

The Law of Attraction

So, you might be asking, "Well, that all sounds well and good, but how in the world do I think, feel, and act in this new way when my life is pretty crappy right now?"

Here's what I have learned in my personal research. Because we are made up of energy, universal source, the Force, whatever you want to call it, we have the power to change our reality within us.

Through his exploration of the ancient writings, scientist and spiritualist, Gregg Braden, spoke of the lost books and texts. He spoke of how much had been edited out of the original biblical work, citing information omitted from what is available today. Religious or not, the information that was left out spans many other teachings.

The language is a bit old school, so I'm going to paraphrase into modern English here. What he found in this example was what we've been told, "Ask and you shall receive," was missing something. The full adage was, "Ask, *then feel it as if it is already here*, and you shall receive." When we feel something as if it's already here, it creates a new energy vibration that attracts what it is you have asked for.

I listened to an interview with world famous talk show host and philanthropist, Oprah Winfrey, and *New York Times best-selling* author, Esther Hicks, on the teachings of Abraham, best understood as a group consciousness from the non-physical realm. Oprah was interviewing Esther on her radio show about how the law of attraction (or law of cause and effect) works. They had been talking for almost half an hour when Esther spoke of an experience where she attracted three things into her life an hour after an interview with a caller and Abraham.

It was in that moment she shared how Abraham explained the law of attraction this way, "When we activate something without resistance, it comes fast." This is where Oprah had one of her signature, "whoa" moments. She loved that and so did I, because it married up with what I had been reading about all this time in such a succinct way.

It also made clear that doubt, worry and struggle are all things that hold us back from seeing the brilliance of who we are. Because, when these things are stronger in our essence than that of joy, freedom, love and anything else positive we want to experience in our lives, the negative energy will "win", for want of a better term.

I could see this in my own life. From a young age, I believed I was a fat person. I struggled with my weight and believed I wasn't good enough because of it. Along the way, I did much personal development work and changed my lifestyle habits, which slowly began to help me shake my belief on this. I was doing OK, but I did still think about my weight quite a lot.

Until something happened that changed it all. It was shortly after I was diagnosed with multiple sclerosis, a disease that can cause damage to the myelin sheaths in the brain and spinal cord, making it difficult for the brain to communicate with parts of the body. I still remember the moment, standing in front of the mirror, looking at myself through new eyes. All the worry and self-talk about being fat stopped. I finally realised that my weight didn't matter, my body was a gift and it was what gave me the ability to walk around and enjoy this world.

From then on, without doing anything else differently, I stopped obsessing about it. I just couldn't do it anymore. And when I stopped, guess what happened? I lost weight. I wasn't huge to begin with, but my old self wouldn't have seen it that way. Now, I eat to nourish myself, and I don't beat myself up if I have some chocolate or some other delicious treat. I simply give it love and enjoy every mouthful. I may still have days when I feel a bit bloated or frumpy (I am human after all), but I don't obsess or worry like I used to. I just accept it and know that it is only a moment. Then I get on with my day.

The blessing of this experience has had a profound effect on me. Not only was the burden of this worry finally released, but it served as a perfect example of how the law of attraction works. The moment I stopped worrying about the weight was the moment I started to drop weight. I was no longer focusing my energy on being fat. I didn't think about it at all and with that, everything seemed to balance. If that isn't an example of how our thoughts, feelings and the law of attraction work, then I don't know what is.

When I thought I was fat, I attracted weight. I was putting the "I'm fat" energy out into the universe. When I stopped thinking about it, the weight came off. Imagine then, if you put your energy, thoughts, feelings and emotions into what you want to attract.

It can't just be a fleeting thought or affirmation we stick on the fridge. If we want to attract that which we desire, we must embody it in every sense of the word. We must *feel* it, we must *ask* for it and we must *believe* it has already happened. In other words, we must also allow for it and *trust* that it is done—whether we can see it with our own eyes or not. It doesn't mean you need to think about it constantly, but when you do, know that it's already here, and keep reaching for uplifting thoughts throughout your day.

Remember what Abraham said in that interview? *"When we activate something without resistance, it comes fast."* Therefore, we must release our limiting beliefs and worries around what it is we truly desire, before it can come forth into our lives. Whether it be healing, creating abundance or attracting love, for example, we must remove resistance.

That said, we must also then learn to let go and trust in the process. If we do not believe in the process, it will not work—because it will simply show you whatever it is you believe.

We can see these limiting beliefs in ourselves and others in many ways. Take money for example. If you were brought up with parents who always said, "Money doesn't grow on trees", or, "We're not made of money", it's likely this story still plays a huge part in where you are financially today. It may have worked in a number of ways. It could have inspired you to work harder than anyone to create a life much different than that of your parents. Or you may still believe this to be true and be in a similar situation to your parents. Alternatively, you may have made money, lost it, made it again and so on, until one day you realised what your limiting belief around money was and finally released it.

So how do we release beliefs that are no longer serving us? How do we get rid of the blocks that are holding us back? What if we are not even aware of these blocks? That's where self-exploration and personal development come in. When we get to know ourselves on a deeper level and see what is holding us back, we can accept our reality, be thankful for the lessons learned and let those negative things go, if indeed we choose to.

Check Point

- What are you accepting and what are you allowing in your life right now?

- If you are here to learn and grow, what are the situations in your life trying to teach you?

- Do you find yourself getting angry at certain people or events taking place in the world? And if you are, what can you do about it? Does it stir up something in you that perhaps needs to be addressed or healed, does it inspire you to want to help and make a difference—or perhaps both?

- What beliefs are you holding onto that, when you stop and think about it, are no longer serving you?

Chapter 3

WHAT ARE YOU WEARING?

How many of us are holding onto things that no longer serve us? Whether we realise it or not, we all do it. We sweep the painful stuff under the rug or hide it deep within, adding yet another layer to the invisible coat we wear.

So what happens when you start to ask questions and ponder your reality? Like any other human on this planet, you can find challenges and opportunities to grow all over the place.

And whilst we may be here to experience the lives and lessons we have chosen, I also believe we are here for something even greater. That is, to help the evolution of the entire universe by raising our energetic vibration through expressing and *being* love—in other words, by shining the brightest we can shine or being the best versions of ourselves.

This is one of the simplest things we can ever do. Yet, for so many of us, it can be the hardest. Why? Because when we come into this world, we have no filter; we are simply a great big ball of unconditional love. We have no judgement, no fear and no understanding of good or bad, or anything else for that matter.

The Unlearning Process

As we grow, we are like sponges. We learn our behaviours, fears and understanding of the world from those who surround us and the environment where we spend most of our time. We learn the things we "should" do and be, what we can and cannot say, how to react and what to believe. We learn who we think we need be, how we should act and how to fit in. For some of us, it can be a great experience. For many of us, though, it can be a mix of some great and some not so great. All of which helps shape who we are today.

It is through all this that we end up wearing our invisible coat. Over time, we add to the layers of beliefs, thoughts and feelings we have developed around ourselves, which can quite frankly weigh us down and hold us back from our greatness. When all we really need to do, is be ourselves. To be our own unique expression of who we came here to be. Not to try and be like anyone else, nor to keep our light dim at the risk of offending others or standing out.

Your role on this planet is to simply be who you are. After all, you are the number one expert at being you. And only you. No one will ever take your place. No one has the exact same path as you, so nothing can ever be taken away from you. Your path is exactly that: yours.

Doesn't it make sense then, no matter where you are in life or what your reality looks like, to begin peeling off the layers of that invisible coat, to discover who you really are? To *be you* is undoubtedly the best thing you can do, for yourself and for all of humanity. You are here to master *your* game. It is why you chose to come here after all.

"But I'm scared! What if when I peel off a layer, all I find is pain?" I look at it this way: when you peel off a layer and find pain, that is your golden opportunity to grow and to let it go. If it is inside you, consciously or not, it is affecting your reality.

Still, for many of us, the thought of having to look at our painful experiences is too much to bear. But to grow, we must do this very thing. It doesn't mean we need to think about the things that were painful for us, day in and day out. It just means we need to acknowledge and accept what happened, forgive those we need to forgive and do the same for ourselves. Only then can we take another step forward in the evolution of who we are.

Underneath the Layers

I'm sure you've heard the saying, "How do you eat an elephant? One bite at a time, of course!" That is such a favourite of mine because it is so true. The analogy of trying to eat the whole thing in one go is just ridiculous and overwhelming. It's the same when it comes to working on ourselves. We can't expect to learn and be enlightened in five minutes. We need to peel off each layer one step at a time.

And if you are here to be all that you can be, facing the reality of your pain might be hard to start with. But once you allow it to teach you what you need to learn, and let go of the suffering it's causing, you will then become lighter and closer to your true self. That is, if you choose to allow it to, of course!

I love the analogy that Wayne Dyer uses to explain this process. When you squeeze an orange, what comes out? Orange juice, right? Would apple juice come out? Vodka, perhaps? That might be nice, but no. When you squeeze the orange, orange juice comes out. It is the same for us humans. When we are tested and squeezed in life, it is our reactions, emotions and feelings that come out.

If you find yourself getting unnecessarily angry when being squeezed, whether the situation is what made you angry or not doesn't change the fact that the anger was inside of you. It wouldn't have come out otherwise, just like the orange. The same can be said for any emotion. Sadness, happiness, joy. It is all a part of you.

The question to then ask yourself is, are these feelings serving me? Perhaps the feelings you choose are appropriate for that moment, nothing more, nothing less.

Sometimes though, there is a lot more to it. Have you ever found yourself overreacting to something in your life? When you think about it, you realise it didn't warrant the blow-up you had or the sadness you felt? That is one of those opportunities to grow. If you ask yourself, what is this truly about? Why did I react that way? Where is this coming from? What do I need to learn here? You are then open to the opportunity for learning that has presented itself.

When you look to find the lesson, it also takes you out of victim mode and puts you back in the driver's seat. For example, if you forever find it hard to make money, what are you and the layers of your coat putting out there? Are you saying out loud or in your mind, "I don't have the money", or, "I can't afford that"? Are you taking responsibility for your life or are you blaming others for the way things are? "Oh, he was supposed to pay me and didn't." "That's because they never pay up." What are you putting out there?

"Alright then, that makes sense, but what if I can't work it out or I have no idea where this is coming from?" That's another great question and perhaps one of the most profound. Why? Because this is where the journey into discovering who you are really begins. If you are asking this question, you are ready to explore yourself at a deeper level.

The best part is, you get to do it any way you choose. Perhaps you'll talk to a counsellor, seek out a holistic doctor, or choose to find a reputable medium or energy healer. Or maybe you'll take up yoga, start meditation or seek out an online personal development course that allows you to do things in your own time and space. Do whatever resonates best with you at the time; it is completely up to you. And as you start to learn and understand yourself at this deeper level, you will open yourself up to shedding yet another layer of that coat you've been wearing all your life, or many lives even.

Personal Growth and Development

As you can probably tell, I am a massive fan of personal growth and development. I honestly think it is one of the most important things we can do for ourselves and others. It doesn't mean I have had it easy, though. On the contrary, some of my biggest, toughest experiences have led to my most profound moments of clarity and understanding. Over the course of my life, I have played the victim, I have attracted situations that mirrored how I felt about myself, and I have allowed people, and my own worries, to get the better of me.

When I was diagnosed with MS in 2013, I had already done much spiritual and personal development work. I had read books, attended events, spoken with a counsellor, completed many personal development courses, listened to experts and learned much about myself along the way.

I even performed the secret letter burn, an exercise a dear friend told me about that I found extremely helpful.

To do this, you need to find a place where you won't be interrupted, where you can write a private letter to one or more people, to tell them exactly how they had made you feel in your life, how it affected you and anything else that comes out. There are no rules or stipulations with this exercise. You just need to write until you can write no more, whether it be one page or 100 pages. When you are finished, you can re-read it if you like, before heading straight to a safe place to burn the letter, so no one except you will ever know what you wrote. Still, it will have been said.

After I did this exercise, I lost three kilos. The aim, of course, wasn't to lose weight. That was simply a side effect that showed me I'd been holding onto everything that was in that letter. Now that I had let it all out, the weight went with it.

When I learned of my MS diagnosis, I was facing yet another of life's challenges, or opportunities to grow. By this stage in my life, I had done enough work to know that I was not the victim here. I didn't think "poor me" or ask "why me?" Had it happened to me 10 years earlier, it may have been a very different story. Instead, I chose to be positive about it.

I told very few people and asked them not to worry, but instead send positive thoughts about healing my way. My family and friends were worried. However, they respected my choice and tried their best to let go of any fear they had and send loving energies my way. And of course, I knew I couldn't tell them how to feel. Their feelings are their own, after all. I just didn't want them to worry and knowing that we are all connected, I didn't want to have any unnecessary fear out in the ether.

What the diagnosis taught me, was that we are always going to be faced with challenges. Sometimes when you think you have dealt with things, you explore even deeper to find that there is still some hurt and pain left. Thus, more room for you to grow.

And that's exactly what happened. A few years after the diagnosis, I attended two courses that would qualify me in Certificate I and II of Emotional Freedom Technique (EFT). This requires tapping on certain acupressure points while talking about a specific event or issue, to help clear it from your energy system. This simple technique has been proven to help with many things, including severe trauma, getting rid of headaches, releasing self-limiting beliefs, and has even been used by veterans of war to help release the symptoms of those who experienced severe PTSD (Post Traumatic Stress Disorder).

In between these courses, I decided to do some one-on-one work with the instructor. I was pondering whether to pursue it beyond the two courses or simply incorporate them into the other modalities I had learned.

I ended up doing about three or four of these sessions. During one particular session, I became very frustrated.

We began working on something I believed I had already cleared! But as the session continued, I found myself working through some deep-seated pain and hurt that led to no less than a good ol' ugly cry (you know the one). The feeling didn't last long, and as we continued the EFT work in that session, my level of hurt and pain dropped from a 10 out of 10, down to a zero. It was as if for that trauma, there was still that last little bit to come out. And come out it certainly did!

The hurt and sadness I allowed myself to feel in that moment and the tears that I shed, helped me to release what was deep inside. It took me a day or so to rebalance but I know it certainly helped me, and I feel much lighter for it.

This example is just one of many opportunities for growth out there. Had this opportunity been presented to me earlier, it may not have had the same impact. A subtle reminder to trust your path and know that you will only ever be confronted by things you can handle. It doesn't mean it will be easy, but if you chose to learn what you need to learn, you will already have the tools to deal with it.

And if you are reading this right now, you have survived 100% of your worst days yet. So give yourself a pat on the back or a high five, for all that you have gone through to get to where you are right now. This human experience of ours isn't always a walk in the park, after all. Although, I believe we are heading that way... but that's a whole other book.

So with all that in mind, how heavy is that invisible coat you are wearing? Is it weighing you down? Are you aware of it? Or are you too afraid to look just yet? Wherever you are, just start there. You get to choose how and when you want to do the work. It is your human experience after all. We'll all be here for the ride with you.

Check Point

If you were completely honest with yourself in evaluating your feelings, how would you answer the following questions?

- Do my feelings serve me?

- Am I overreacting to something that doesn't warrant the anger or sadness I feel?

- What is this about? Why did I react that way? Where is this coming from?

- What do I need to learn here?

Secret Letter Burn

Are you interested in doing the secret letter burn for yourself? Find a private, quiet place where you won't be interrupted, grab yourself a pen and some sheets of paper, then pour out everything you want to say to a person or to multiple people. When it is all out, make sure you are in a safe place, then burn the letter.

Chapter 4

HEADS OR TAILS

Perhaps a better name for this chapter would be "heads *and* tails". Why? Well, you can't have one without the other. You can certainly toss a coin and have it land so that either heads or tails shows, but whichever way the coin lands, the other side will still exist. What a brilliant analogy this is to explain life.

For a long time, understanding wholeness and "being one" confused me. I couldn't understand how we could be whole and connected when so many bad things seem to happen in the world. So much suffering, so many mistakes made by us all.

One day the whole coin analogy sunk in. Call me a slow learner but I got there in the end. It makes sense, doesn't it? You, me and everyone on this planet, including the planet itself, is whole. We aren't half an Earth. There isn't half a sun and we aren't half a person, no matter our size or make up.

Love and Fear

So just like the coin, we each have two sides at any given time. It is in this contrast, the duality of our human experience, that we can discern for ourselves what is and what isn't at any given moment. Unless you were wrapped up in cotton wool and never, ever made a mistake or a choice you wish you could change, you will have experienced both sides of the coin in your life.

You have loved, you have hated. You have been happy, you have been sad. You have felt lost, you have felt found. You have been scared, you have been empowered. All these things boil down to love or fear. You choose which one in any given moment of your reality.

Fear can look like various things. Keep in mind, there is a difference between fear and danger. Danger (or "danger fear") is when your body reacts, to let you know that there is something hazardous that you must avoid—like running away from a grizzly bear or standing very still in the presence of a snake so that it won't bite.

Day-to-day fear, on the other hand, is different. It's the feeling you get when you're about to do something extremely challenging, confronting or new. Take public speaking as an example. A grizzly bear isn't going to attack you while you stand on stage and deliver your words. However, fear can certainly be present. The thing is though, you have the power to choose how you will let the fear affect you. Will you let it debilitate you? Or will you let it kick you in the direction of your dreams? The choice is yours.

As writer and entrepreneur, Seth Godin, once said, "If it scares you, it might be a good thing to try."

Or, as Susan Jeffers says throughout her book and in its title, "Feel the fear and do it anyway."

Okay, back to the whole coin analogy. As you can see, when you look at things this way, it is easier to see why there are opposites of everything; that is, two sides to the coin. Without it in fact, there would be no contrast. We would not be aware of day or night, good or bad, hot or cold.

Therefore, we need to love and honour everything, not just the good bits. Why? Because we aren't only happy all the time. We aren't just blissful all the time. And whilst we can aim for this to be our reality, anyone who has ever been human knows that sometimes, life will throw you a curve ball and you will need to deal with some heavy stuff. That, whatever your reality, is life.

It Takes Time

I love what spiritual teacher, speaker and best-selling author, Marianne Williamson, often says when talking about human suffering and sadness. Imagine you have fallen over and scraped your knee. Blood is rushing out and is everywhere. The wound is quite deep and you may or may not need stitches. You will, however, require time for it to heal. During this time, the blood will clot, a scab will be formed and eventually fall off, perhaps leaving a small scar behind.

Going through a tough time in your life is absolutely no different. For some reason though, we often think we have to show only the good, happy side of our coin to the world—especially when it comes to social media. We think we shouldn't be sad for long.

This leads many people to feel depressed, anxious and alone, not understanding that the grieving process is exactly that: a process. We must go through it as part of our healing. Does that mean it will be easy? Maybe not. But the healing needs to occur. We aren't here to experience just one side of the coin. That would be like going to the cinema and only watching half the movie or just the good bits.

Being able to appreciate, love and accept both sides of who we are allows us to be *whole*. Sure there are values, morals and many other things to consider. Our aim definitely isn't to go around doing bad things on purpose. However, acceptance allows us to more easily forgive ourselves and others for things that have caused pain. When we operate out of fear instead of love, we are more likely to hurt ourselves and others the most. Ultimately, when we do not forgive, we only hurt ourselves.

As best-selling self-help author, coach and teacher, Debbie Ford, explains in the movie, *The Shadow Effect*, when you embrace all that you are, you are truly free.

Famous 18th century British author, Alexander Pope, put it this way, "To err is human, to forgive, divine."

Knowing that we are connected—I am one whole coin, you are another—and our planet, Mother Earth, is one giant coin we inhabit—it stands to reason that our thoughts, feelings and consciousness affect everyone and everything on some scale, either positively or negatively. That is why to heal the world starts by healing yourself. It doesn't feel like such a mammoth task then, does it? If we were all to do this for ourselves, imagine the possibilities!

You Have the Power

When you send love to yourself, you are sending love to everyone. When you beat up on yourself for not being good enough, you create a negative vibration. And when you hate on others who do not fit in with your belief system, you are sending that.

If you want to see a better world, then it really does start with you. You have the power within you. It is that simple, yet for so many of us, it is so hard.

Even as an advocate for personal growth and development, I didn't always understand how working on myself could positively affect the entire planet. It isn't just us humans we can positively affect, either. It is the plants, the weather, our oceans, the flowers, the animals—everything.

How many times have you seen on the news, something horrible happen in one place in the world, like a mass shooting or some other form of violence, only to see a huge natural disaster at almost the very same time on the other side of the world?

Not only does this show we are all connected but also the law of cause and effect in full flight. Some may call it a coincidence, but this law is fact. And knowing that we are all connected, these events, natural disasters, extreme weather changes—we have all played our part in it.

Our mission then, if we are to heal the planet? Rather than sending hate, wishing things weren't the way they were and focusing on what isn't right from our point of view, we need only send love to others and ourselves.

If you have never thought this way before, it might sound a bit weird or "woo-woo". But this is our choice. This is our human experience. If in your reality, you want to create more love, then you know what to do. And if you see things a different way, that is your choice, too.

At the end of the day, you can't have one without the other; no love without hate, no light without dark. It's how we know what is what. Therefore, it is your choice to interpret each thing, each event, each moment in time, your way. Everything just *is* until you put meaning to it. It is your choice how you respond. It is your reality.

Check Point

- When looking at both sides of the coin of your life, what would you prefer to sweep under the rug? Is there room for healing, acceptance or forgiveness?

- What are you ready or willing to let go of?

Chapter 5

WHAT YOU SEE IS WHAT YOU GET

For a long time, I believed my legs were fat and horrible. I knew deep down they weren't *that* bad, but because of this engrained belief, I was never confident enough to wear shorts. I felt, for the shape of my legs (at all the different sizes they have been), shorts just didn't work. They would ride up my crotch, and I would feel gross and agitated.

One year though, something happened. I can't tell you exactly what it was but I finally decided I would wear shorts. I know to many people, this may be the weirdest thing they have ever heard—especially considering I live in one of the driest, hottest places on the planet and have been to so many outdoor music festivals, in pants, in summer. Even when it was 46 degrees Celsius. (I know, I know—what the?)

The Year of Shorts

When I had this mindset shift, one that I can't explain, except for maybe the wisdom of getting older and knowing that it really doesn't matter, I declared it "The Year of Shorts".

I remember going to my hairdresser and good friend around the time of this declaration. We were chatting away when I asked her, "What is your year going to be about?" We had talked about how some people pick a word for the year ahead like "abundance", "creative", or "wealth". My hairdresser had picked something quite empowering for her and we spoke about what it would mean for her year ahead.

Then she asked me and I of course exclaimed proudly, "This year is the year of shorts!"

She looked at me and then we both began to crack up. For ages, with tears of laughter rolling down our faces.

When my hairdresser could finally speak again, she said, "I thought you were going to say something insightful or inspiring, but no, the year of shorts!" to which we proceeded to laugh for another five minutes.

I then remember going for a walk with a dear friend I have known since I was 10 years old. I was in shorts. She couldn't believe it. "Ned," she said (my nickname), "I can't believe you have not worn shorts for all of these years. Every festival, every hot day. Finally!"

I knew how crazy it was and so did she. This belief that I could never wear shorts and expose my legs, had been learned so young and reinforced by not-so-rad boyfriends, comparisons and society throughout my youth. It had arrived at a place so deep inside of me, so etched into my body, its energy and all that I was, it took years to expose and let go.

How many of us are holding onto beliefs that are just as silly as this one? I don't profess to be some supermodel with long, luscious legs, but I know how limiting it has been to hold onto something so tightly. More importantly, I understand why I was holding onto this belief because I was willing to explore myself at a deeper level. I was willing to accept my reality and finally let go.

What about you? What are you holding onto that may not actually be true for you anymore?

Your Beliefs

When we were little, we were who we were. As we got older, people didn't expect us to remain who we were at age 5, 10 or even 20 years old. Why do we hang onto things that defined us as youths? We don't walk around in the same clothes, so why walk around with the same views?

Famous boxer, Muhammad Ali, once said, "If you are still thinking the same at 50 as you were at 20, you have wasted 30 years of your life."

It makes sense, doesn't it? Why operate your life on a set of beliefs and standards that are no longer relevant or serving you in a way that benefits your highest good?

If you recognise these things about yourself, get brave and explore who you are, how do you get rid of something so deeply engrained? And, being that your body is made up of energy that needs to flow freely, any ailments, pain and emotional baggage you hold will create blockages of energy that need to be released.

Sometimes, you will be aware of these blocks and sometimes, not.

I remember working with a friend who was getting ready to have her first baby. She was excited and couldn't wait to be a mum. In the lead-up to the birth, she had been reading a book about tapping (EFT). She explained what she had learned from the book, and that when she went into labour, she would start tapping to take away the pain.

I remember doing the one eyebrow raise in my head thinking, "You are going to be pushing a giant watermelon out of your hoo-jar, how the hell will tapping take that pain away?"

In hindsight, I think the tapping would have been more for bringing down her anxiety. And today, having had my own positive experience with EFT, this whole tapping thing makes a lot more sense.

In fairness, this was many years ago now. However, the fact remains that I once thought tapping was a load of hogwash. Seriously, how could you tap on a point on your body and reduce anxiety? Even with all the personal development I had done up to that point, this was not something I was picking up or putting down.

Fast forward to today, and it's a whole other story. Not only have I used tapping, or EFT (Emotional Freedom Technique, as it is officially called). I have studied it and experienced for myself the power simply tapping on a few acupressure points can have, to help relieve pain, anxiety, trauma, anger, sadness and overwhelm. Not only that, I have used it to promote positive feelings of energy, insight, deeper intuition and lightness within myself.

EFT is just one example of something I once thought was silly, to something that has become an awesome tool in my personal development toolkit of life. It is also a perfect example of "now you see it, now you don't", or the other way around.

Think about it. When you were five years old, did you believe in the tooth fairy? Did you get all excited when you saw that coin under your pillow the morning after losing your tooth? Do you believe it now?

Of course not. So why do we stay so rigid in many of our beliefs? Where did we learn them, and who taught us anyway? Our beliefs are just that: beliefs, not facts. We are the ones who give things meaning. Without that meaning, it all just *is*. No words. No judgement. No meaning.

What are some beliefs that you have been holding onto, perhaps unconsciously, that you may be ready or willing to let go? Notice I say ready or willing? Sometimes we might be very ready to let something go. Other times, it might be too hard, too fresh or too raw. In that case, we simply need to be willing to let go until we become ready to let go.

The thing is, you can't let go of what you're not aware of, or don't acknowledge. It is like the alcoholic who cannot see they have a problem; the obese person who doesn't see the harm in not exercising and eating a diet full of saturated fat and sugar; or the gambler who tries his luck just once more every day in case he wins this time. Until they admit to themselves that they need help or have a problem, they will not be able to make a change.

It is the same for all of us. Some circumstances are more extreme than others but essentially the same, nonetheless.

Over the years, I have had many addictions and low phases in my life. From smoking and eating crappy food, to an eating disorder, partying, drinking, constantly worrying, being ridiculously hard on myself, treating my body like absolute crap and not caring much about myself at all.

Whilst I have worked very hard to get to where I am today, with some of these phases being shorter than others, everything, every action, every uncaring attitude—all comes back to feelings of not being good enough, shame, guilt, anger and fear. And even though there are so many amazing qualities and beliefs instilled in me and all of us for that matter, the painful parts tend to trip us up the most. But it's also from these parts that we learn our best lessons, which in turn serve as our biggest gifts—if we choose to let them.

Check Point

- What beliefs are you holding onto that may not be true for you anymore?

- Do you have any symptoms that may be highlighting the need to do some deeper work on understanding and releasing your blockages?

- What are you ready to let go of?

- What one thing are you willing to look at in your life right now that may be worth considering from a different point of view?

Chapter 6

KNOW BETTER, DO BETTER?

A few years ago, a good friend of mine sent me a Facebook message saying she'd just had a past life session, or QHHT (Quantum Healing Hypnosis Therapy) session, as it is formally known. She said it was with a lady who was amazing and I had to try it for myself. Whilst I had done a lot of different things at that point, this was something I had never before considered. But with a recommendation like that, I called and booked on the spot. I didn't give it a second thought—it was almost as though my intuition had made the phone call. Whatever the case, I am so grateful I made that appointment.

I ended up having three different sessions over the space of a couple of years and learned a lot about myself. I also gained a most beautiful new friend for life, Sonia. She and I are the same age, and to me she is like an amazon goddess with beauty that radiates both inside and out.

I remember at one of our catch ups, Sonia said something so insightful, I will never forget it. I was speaking about how in the past, I had indeed known better than to do silly things like smoke and treat my body very un-like a temple, for example. But for some reason, I still did them. I wasn't sticking to the famous quote by Maya Angelou: "Do the best you can until you know better. Then when you know better, do better," which I had paraphrased to Sonia as, "When you know better, you do better."

I was beating myself up as this "know better, do better" quote obviously didn't seem to work with me. When Sonia replied, "Perhaps the quote should really be, 'when you know *yourself* better, you can do better.'"

Dang! Light bulbs went off everywhere! This slight change made a quote I already loved so much better. Sonia was right. It isn't until we know *ourselves* better that we can understand why we do what we do, including these silly things sometimes—and the great things, too, of course.

That front of mind, the exploration of ourselves, our own personal development journey, is paramount if we want to move forward, grow and evolve. To know ourselves better helps us to understand who we really are.

Acceptance

A side-shoot of that is then self-love and acceptance. We know that we can't accept what we don't acknowledge. And that only when the student is ready, will the teacher appear. I bet you can think of some moments, words, people or experiences that have helped shape your life— if the timing for those moments or words of wisdom had happened at any other time, perhaps they would not have been as insightful. Perhaps you would not have been ready to hear the message. Perhaps you would not have taken from it all that you did in that moment.

Those words, that insight from Sonia, profoundly helped shape my understanding of myself and others. In my reality, this has been such a gift.

As I continue to explore myself and all that is, I have noticed that not everyone shares the same vision of exploration for themselves. Not everyone wants to explore. If you are someone like me, who finds the human experience fascinating, with a thirst to discover more, you may not understand why others are not interested in doing the same. The thing to remember here is that not everyone is ready. Nor does everyone want a deeper discovery to be part of their reality, in any case.

I believe we have all come to this amazing planet to learn different lessons and to be part of the game in different ways. Some of us are ready to explore, while others may walk a different path. Neither experience is better than the other, just different.

Knowing this is so empowering. It allows me to understand why we are all where we are. None of it is a mistake, it is simply a choice we have made—either before coming through or along the way.

While we may have come here to learn, it is important to remember that we also have free will. We have the power to choose who we want to be, how we want to feel and what we want to think, at any given moment. Therefore, the future, whether loosely written or not, is up to us.

Awesome, isn't it? We can create our own reality. We are that extraordinary. Yet how often do we forget this? It is so easy to, after all. What with bills, work, kids, friends, our stuff, events—the list goes on. We are constantly bombarded with so much, that to cut through the noise and remember who we are can sometimes prove difficult.

So how do we combat this? If we look at the whole "know *yourself* better, do better" analogy, we can start with looking at our own life. What is working and what isn't? Where are you spending the bulk of your time? What gives you the most value, love and joy?

Next, you can start tapping into yourself further to develop your intuition, so you can make better decisions that make sense for you. You may do this through meditation, journaling, walks along the beach, spending time with like-minded people or attending personal development events in person or online. Whatever the case, the more you strengthen your intuition and your relationship with yourself, the more discerning you will become, and the easier it will be for you to play the game the way you want to.

You will also be able to notice old patterns that keep showing up in your life. By looking at them through a different lens, your perspective and understanding change. Like Wayne Dyer once said, "Change the way you look at things and the things you look at will change."

It's simple, isn't it? Why do we insist on making life so hard sometimes?

Check Point

- What are you willing to look at from a different point of view in your life right now?

- When it comes to developing your intuition and deepening your relationship with yourself, which of the following activities appeal to you? Meditation, journaling, getting outdoors and being with nature, spending time with like-minded people, attending personal development events in person or online, practicing mindfulness or something else?

- What one thing can you do to cut through the noise and find time to examine your life?

- What is working in the life of you? What isn't?

- Where do you spend the bulk of your time?

- What gives the you most value, love and joy?

Chapter 7

GOOD VIBRATIONS

When listening to that interview I spoke about in Chapter 2 with Oprah and Esther Hicks, I was interested to learn about a significant discovery that Jerry Hicks, Esther's late husband, had made. He'd been a long-time fan of the inspirational classic, *Think and Grow Rich*, by Napoleon Hill. Jerry had read the book cover-to-cover too many times to count, referencing much of the book's information when running workshops and teaching his students.

During the interview, Esther spoke of a story that led Jerry to discover the original manuscript of this book. Upon this discovery, Jerry carefully compared the manuscript to the original book published in 1937.

After doing my own research, I too discovered what Jerry had found. It's fascinating. In the original manuscript, Napoleon Hill used the word "vibration". As far as I can tell, although the word may appear sporadically in the book published in 1937, the word was still edited out a further 37 times. Within the published book, Napoleon

Hill referred to this as "the secret". And whilst the title alludes to it, there is of course more to it.

We Are Creators

We already know that thoughts become things and are therefore made up of energy. This energy then attracts what we put into the universe, consciously or not. We also know that energy is everywhere, in all that we do and are. So not only do our thoughts become things, but so do our emotions, feelings, beliefs and actions: everything.

Of the many references Napoleon Hill shares in his book, here are just a few that I found interesting and insightful.

"The ether in which this little earth floats, in which we move and have our being, is a form of energy moving at an inconceivably high rate of vibration, and that the ether is filled with a form of universal power which ADAPTS itself to the nature of the thoughts we hold in our minds; and INFLUENCES us, in natural ways, to transmute our thoughts into their physical equivalent."*

"THOUGHTS WHICH ARE MIXED WITH ANY OF THE FEELINGS OF EMOTIONS, CONSTITUTE A "MAGNETIC" FORCE WHICH ATTRACTS, FROM THE VIBRATIONS OF THE ETHER, OTHER SIMILAR, OR RELATED THOUGHTS."*

"The ether is a great cosmic mass of eternal forces of vibration. It is made up of both destructive vibrations and constructive vibrations. It carries, at all times, vibrations of fear, poverty, disease, failure, misery; and vibrations of prosperity, health, success, and happiness, just as surely as it carries the sound of hundreds of orchestrations of music, and hundreds of human voices, all of which maintain their own individuality, and means of identification, through the medium of radio."*

Some say the word vibration was edited out of the book because it was believed that it would be more marketable this way. Either way, what Napoleon Hill speaks of in his book is not a stand-alone example. Energy and the way it works is discussed much more these days and is widely accepted. In saying that, we sometimes forget, become distracted, or simply don't take the time to explore it further.

Unconditional Love

When I read Anita Moorajani's first book, *Dying to be Me*, she explained what she believed to be true and the purpose of life after having a near death experience (NDE) in February of 2006. Anita had a cultured upbringing, and like all of us, learned about the world through her experiences and the people around her.

Anita has a loving husband, Danny—the type of guy she never thought she would be with, especially after the poor relationships she had prior to meeting him. In her book, she tells the story of both her father and dear friend dying from cancer. Then one day, Anita was diagnosed with the same thing.

She went to great lengths to become healthy and beat the cancer. However, her body began to shut down until eventually she ended up in hospital, in a coma. It was during this time that she had her near-death experience.

Anita described this experience as best she could, stating that words just didn't seem to do it justice. She wrote of the unconditional love she felt during her experience. She understood that all she needed to do while in her human body was be exactly who she was. In other words, as she says in her book and to audiences all over the globe, all you need to do is be you—and remember that you are loved.

I love this analogy Anita uses to describe what she learned about who we really are. Imagine you are standing in the middle of a giant warehouse, only the lights are off. It is pitch black, and you have only a torchlight to see by. In any given moment, you can only see what the light shines upon. Now, imagine this is the only way you know. Until one day, the lights to the entire warehouse are switched on and finally you can see everything that is there. It is indescribably beautiful, you see colours you didn't know existed and you hear sounds you have never heard before. It is magnificent.

Our life is what we see with the torchlight only. Everything else is there, we just can't see it with our own eyes. But it does not mean it doesn't exist.

When Anita chose to come back into her physical body, she came back with the understanding of all that is. She had been the person who once only saw with the torchlight. Then she got a glimpse and understanding of all that is, with all the warehouse lights turned on. And then she came back—with the knowledge of what the entire warehouse looked like—to life where the torchlight was the norm.

Anita's experience can be likened to that of a rubber band being stretched for the first time. It can never go back to its original size once stretched. When you think about it, we have all had experiences like this. Maybe not to this extreme, but experiences just the same.

Perhaps you learned or unlearned something. Perhaps something that was true for you turned out to be the complete opposite. No matter the example, your thoughts about that thing will never be the same.

After reading Anita's story, I became curious about other people's NDEs. I certainly knew I didn't need to have one. I just wanted to see if what she spoke about was similar to other people's experiences. I have found that whilst what happens on "the other side" is slightly different for each individual, the one thing in common is the unconditional love they felt when they were there; not to mention the knowingness of all that is. People also spoke of there being no judgement, no worry and no fear. Each person came out of the experience with the understanding that we are all indeed connected and who we really are is magnificent beyond comprehension.

Dr. Eben Alexander, renowned academic neurosurgeon based in the US, experienced an NDE and wrote about it in his book, *Proof of Heaven*. When he was on "the other side", he only needed to *feel* where he desired to be and, in an instant, he was there.

Interestingly, since there is no judgment, fear, emotional baggage or self-limiting thoughts of any kind, Dr. Alexander's experience shows us that it was *feeling*, not thought, that granted him the ability to create his own reality instantly in that realm—the ether that we, too, are a part of.

Knowing this, even if this sort of thing stretches your mind a bit, serves as a reminder of our wholeness and connection to all that is. And that we are indeed powerful beings, with the ability to create our reality in a way that works for us. Our experience as humans then, hanging out on this lil' ol' planet of ours, isn't that the miracle?

Intention

Tony Robbins says, "Where energy goes, energy flows." With the understanding that we are all connected, doesn't it make so much sense that if you want more love, you must have love for yourself? If you want more hope, you must first be hopeful. If you want more of anything, you must first be that. It is the law of attraction. It is the way energy works. It is the way vibration works. It is the way you work!

If we have the power to attract what it is we desire through thought, feeling, belief and emotion, what is to stop us from healing ourselves? We already know it is possible. In an example shared on YouTube and explained by Gregg Braden (referenced at the end of this book), we watch as a tumour in a woman at a medicine-less hospital in China, simply disappears. Loosely translated, the words that are being spoken by the three physicians performing the removal of the tumour are "already done" and "now". It is important to note, and as Gregg mentions when explaining the experience, that the words themselves are not so important. It is the thoughts, in addition to the feelings, that are. What is key here is the feeling the physicians hold, as if it has already happened—that the tumour has disappeared. There is also no judgement present whatsoever. The tumour is neither good nor bad. The physicians simply use thought, feeling—and I would add belief and intention—which in turn sees the tumour removed. The process itself takes only three minutes.

This is just one example, one of many I am sure. And one that when it comes down to it, is up to you to decide whether you will allow for this to be true in your reality.

When we see something like this in action, whatever our personal belief system, it reminds us that we are quite powerful, amazing creatures. Throughout his life and in his books, Wayne Dyer reminds us of the power of the two words "I am" because whatever follows these two words, creates an energy vibration of thought and feeling.

This leads to either a positive feeling or a negative one. For example, self-talk such as "I am such a failure", "I am a loser", "I am so fat", "I am so broke", or "I am so lonely" creates a feeling that you are not good enough and will never have enough. If we consider that to attract what it is we deeply desire, we must then act *as if* it has already occurred and trust that it is done, rather than using self-talk to create feelings of what we don't want; we must instead reach for words, feelings, emotions and actions that help to create what we do want.

Even if we don't know what we want, reaching for words and feelings that encourage positive feelings will surely provide benefit. For example, you could use words like, "I am ready to see what I want", "I am loved", "I am safe", "All is well", "Good things come to me", "Miracles happen every day", or, "I am truly blessed".

Gandhi once said, "We must be the change we wish to see in the world." We must *be* the change we wish to see. There's that feeling of "as if" again! To be the change, we must feel we are already the change that we seek. We must act as if it is already in our existence. We must imagine it, set an intention for it, ask for it and be all that it is. Just like a magnet attracts, we need only remember that we, too, are a magnet.

Now I am not saying that we will *always* be able to get all that we desire, as I do believe that some things just aren't meant to be, that there are lessons we must learn along the way and as we all know, life happens. However, when it comes down to it, the way you tackle your own game of life, and how you see things in it at any given moment, is still your choice. You can choose to think, act, feel and be in one way or another, with conscious creation and awareness, or not. Either way, you attract what you embody and believe at any given moment of your reality.

Without wanting to sound like a broken record, isn't loving yourself, releasing your blocks, identifying the patterns in your life that are no longer serving you, accepting what is so you can move forward, being authentically *you* and being grateful for all that you have right now, the best thing you can do to experience your greatness and fullness? What intention do you want to set for yourself? What is it that you want to attract? How do you want to feel?

You are powerful beyond measure. What you choose to do with your power is completely up to you. All you need to keep in mind is, what you put out there, you get back. If perhaps nothing else, do what Ellen DeGeneres says at the end of each show: "Be kind to one another." I believe it is a perfect place to start.

Check Point

- What intention do you want to set for yourself?

- What do you want to attract?

- How do you want to feel?

Chapter 8

THE RELATIONSHIP FACTOR

Ah, relationships. Fascinating, aren't they? Think of all the relationships you have in your life right now—from the closest, to the people at your grocery store. What are they like? How do you interact with these people? Who do you find yourself acting differently with? What do you learn from these relationships? Who is the teacher? Who is the student?

As we have discovered, our reality reflects all that we are. Therefore, it stands to reason that we learn the most through our relationships. Whether it's through ourselves, our loved ones, work colleagues, strangers, nature or our pets, every relationship is there to heal us, teach us or help us in some way.

Quite often, it is the most painful relationships and uncomfortable experiences that grow us the most. They can either leave us more compassionate or bitter. From the person who was endlessly bullied at school, who makes a conscious decision to never be that mean to anyone because they know how horrible it feels—to the person who was beaten as a child, who repeats the pattern as an adult. Each experience leads to another, shaping who you are. How you let it shape you is up to you. Whether you make the choice consciously or not, it is part of your reality.

So how is it that our relationships teach us about ourselves? Well they are a reflection of what we think about ourselves in our reality. There are many ways this works. My understanding of how each relationship teaches us and evolves our soul has certainly come from my own experience. From attracting people who treated me badly because I believed I was not good enough, to attracting amazing people as I began to love myself.

If you are human, which I am guessing you are, no doubt you have experienced some painful and perhaps some exhilarating lessons through your relationships. When thinking about this, is there anyone who was in your life for a while, but is no longer? Is it obvious what they were there for? What did you learn from them? What do you think they learned from you? Were you the teacher, the student, or both?

Understanding the power of our relationships and why they exist allows for a whole new perspective. If you can detach and look at your relationships with the intention of understanding the purpose, what can you see? Rather than saying, "Why is this happening to me?" or, "Why does this *always* happen to me in my relationships?" instead ask, "What is this relationship trying to teach me? What do I need to learn?" If you are still unclear, write down or say out loud, "I want to understand" or, "I am willing to understand, please show me what it is I need to know." Again, only if this is something you wish to integrate into that reality of yours.

I have always been fascinated with relationships, particularity as I better understood what they were for. Some are for the lessons, others are to teach or learn and some are simply there for a bloody good time—to share in joy, love and to laugh our faces off!

Over the years, I have noticed that some people can rub you up the wrong way. What I found though is, often the 'thing' that tends to grind your gears the most, is actually something you do yourself and are not even aware of.

My mum taught me this (not that I was happy about it at the time, as it meant looking in the mirror), and it was a great introduction into one of the ways relationships can help us with our own evolution. As I continued to research the topic over the years, I found Gregg Braden explains it quite well through his study and research.

The Seven Essence Mirrors

As mentioned earlier, Gregg Braden is a scientist and spiritualist who has done much exploration on relationships and the way they shape us. He has travelled to many amazing places, lived with indigenous tribes and explored places many of us can only dream of. In his adventures and through his research, he has discerned what he feels the ancient Essences were trying to teach through the "Seven Essence Mirrors".

Whilst I have not read the ancient scriptures myself, my learnings from Gregg have provided me with much insight when it comes to relationships. And whether you subscribe to any religion or dogma, or call yourself spiritual or not, the way the mirrors are explained certainly provide great grounds for exploring who we really are, to broaden our scope of self-awareness.

I believe we are all here to teach each other and to learn in the same way. It is our relationships that provide the contrast in our reality, to help us to discern who we are, what we believe, where we should focus our time and energy, how to love, how to live and what we are here for. All of these things help shape our reality.

That said, if we look at this through the lens of the Seven Essence Mirrors, through Gregg's research (something I continue to explore for myself, too), we can see that our relationships may be teaching us many a lesson at any given time. Each "mirror" providing an opportunity to learn through what is reflected back to ourselves from others.

The First Mirror

This first mirror relates to our presence in the moment. It reflects who we are in any given moment. That is, our internal reality, in an instant. It is mirroring our joy, our anger, our love, our emotion, our vibe. Whatever it is we are radiating in that moment. This is what my mum was talking about when I was annoyed by someone else's behaviour, it was because I actually did the same thing.

The Second Mirror

The second mirror is similar, only rather than reflecting what we are in that moment, it reflects what we *judge* in that moment. It reflects something we have an emotional charge with, that perhaps stems from an experience we had in the past and/or may not have yet healed or forgiven. While it may be beneficial to be shown this mirror to ensure we don't "go down that track again" so to speak, should we judge and condemn with strong emotion, we will then, as the law of attraction states, attract more of what we judge into our life. If we can make peace with it, however, the mirror for that particular experience will stop showing up. In other words, the lesson we needed to learn will have been learnt.

The Third Mirror

The third mirror reflects back to us something we may have lost, given away or had taken away from us in another person. Often we may find ourselves attracted to others who we feel have something we don't—something we once had but lost, gave away or had stolen from us when were likely quite young. This could be anything —love, innocence, honesty, understanding, respect, joy or courage for, example. The great news is, once you recognise this, you can take steps to reclaim whatever it may be within yourself and begin to heal.

The Fourth Mirror

The fourth mirror allows us to see ourselves in the presence of addiction or compulsion. During our lives we will adopt patterns of behaviour. These patterns become important to us, and because they have been part of our reality for so long, we often feel as though "it is all we know". Through these patterns and behaviours, we over time give our power away, sometimes even losing the things we love most.

Whilst some addictions or compulsions may be obvious, like smoking or drinking, others may be less obvious, like control issues or the need to be perfect all the time.

When this mirror shows up in your life, it allows you to see things as they really are, providing you with the perfect opportunity to forgive, heal and release the old pattern or behaviour.

The Fifth Mirror

This very subtle mirror is the one that our parents show us through the course of our lives. This mirror asks us to allow for the possibility that maybe it is our parents—through their own actions and behaviours—who are mirroring our own expectations for ourselves and others and from others back to us, as well as our beliefs about source energy, the divine, God, The Force, whatever you prefer to call it.

Gregg explains it with this example. Let's say you find yourself in a relationship where you are judged constantly by your mother and/or father, or that you feel your best is never good enough. There is a high probability that within that relationship, the truth of what is being reflected by this mirror is your belief within yourself that you may not be good enough, or that you haven't accomplished what was expected of you through your perception of yourself and your creators.

As Gregg relays, this mirror, whilst extremely subtle, may provide us with the most wisdom of all when it comes to why we have lived our lives the way we have. It may also be the reason some of us tend to attract partners who have the same attributes as our mothers or fathers, too.

The Sixth Mirror

This mirror is sometimes referred to as the "dark night of the soul". In saying that, it doesn't necessarily mean the sh*t is going to hit the fan. What is does do though, is remind us that life has a way of balancing things out in the same way nature does. When we find ourselves in the greatest challenges of life, it is important to remember that the only way these challenges are even possible is because we have been gathering the tools, wisdom and understandings throughout our lives to confront them.

In essence, we are never given more than we can handle. The challenge simply would not be happening in our lives otherwise. How we react to these challenges, or opportunities, is of course completely up to us. This mirror also provides an opportunity for us to demonstrate to ourselves our own mastery and to show us that the process of life may be trusted.

The Seventh Mirror

This mirror is often the most subtle and difficult. It requires us to allow for the possibility that no matter the outcome of each experience, it is perfect in its nature—regardless of whether or not we have achieved our goals. This mirror calls for us to look at ourselves without comparison, without judgement, and to see ourselves and all that is as perfect.

This last mirror reminds me of something Anita Moorjani says when speaking about her NDE. When she was in the experience she could choose whether to go back to her physical body or to stay, explaining that whatever her decision, it would be perfect.

As you reflect upon these mirrors and what they mean for you, what do you notice? I am not here to discern whether this resonates with you or not of course, that choice is always yours and yours only.

Check Point

If looking at your relationships in this way appeals to you, here are some questions you might like to consider.

- Of the people who have been part of your life in some way or another up until this point, is it obvious what they were there for? What did you learn from them? What do you think they learned from you? Were you the teacher, the student, or both?

- If you look at your current relationships through the eyes of wanting to understand their purpose, what can you see? What are these relationships trying to teach you? What do you think you need to learn?

- As you reflect upon these mirrors and what they mean for you, what do you notice? How are you evolving? What kind of people or situations keep showing up in your life? What might you need to let go of? Are there any patterns you notice? What are you willing to see?

Chapter 9

ARE YOU WILLING TO EXPLORE?

As I have said throughout these pages, your reality is exactly that: yours. You create it, and you allow it to shape the person you are, no matter the experience. Knowing all you know then—that you really are that powerful—the question remains, are you willing to explore?

I have been in bands for much of my life as a singer and songwriter. In one song, I wrote about this exact question. In another, I wrote the following lyric, "Life brings you back again, until you learn the lesson, life brings you back somehow, until you see all that you need to, until your truth is found."

Exploring who I am and this thing we call life has always fascinated me. In saying that, it has not always been sexy, happy, enlightening or fun. Sometimes it has been darn painful and hard. That said, I wouldn't change it. As challenging as some of my experiences have been, they have taught me so much about myself and life. Had I not gone through all that I have, I may not have started my own businesses and met the same incredible people, not to mention have the outlook on life that I do. It is priceless, and for that, I am deeply grateful.

As I said in the introduction, my thoughts and insights on life are based on all that I know and feel. It is the truth of my reality at the time of writing this. I know, based on what I have learned up until this point, that my views may indeed change after this book has been published, read and re-published. That's okay; we are evolving creatures after all, here on this beautiful planet, learning as we go!

I often say to myself and others, "Wow, I have seriously learned so much in the past ten years. Imagine what the next ten years will hold! Imagine how much more I will have learned!"

At the core of it all, you are love. We all are. We are not here to destroy each other, but to lift each other up, to bring humanity into a place where we all experience the fullness of each and every moment. I don't want this to sound airy fairy. I'm not talking about rainbows and lolly pops (but by all means, if that is what rings your bells, sure!).

However, as we begin to explore and remove all the crap that has slowly suffocated us over the years, if we let go of how things are "supposed to be", according to mass media or what we've been told, and if we drop into our hearts, tap into our intuition, inner knowing, gut feeling, pray—or whatever it is for us—then perhaps we will see that life *is* the miracle and that our moment in time is the greatest gift of all.

We can see that our part isn't just to sit and take it all in (although I believe this is a huge part). Our role is to ensure that we, as a collective consciousness, get to sit back and take it all in for eternity. The beauty of it all. The miracle of life.

Trust the Process

Where do you start with all of this then? You simply start where you are. Be willing and open. Trust that what you need to let go of will surface, but only if and when you are ready or willing to do the work.

The more you let go, the lighter you become, the more compassionate you become, the more self-aware you become, the more you can see yourself in a new light and allow yourself to shine.

You weren't put here to be a second-rate version of yourself. You are here to be the best version of you that you can be. And if we consider the Seventh Mirror, you are already perfect. Everything is. Over the years though, you may have added layer upon layer of limiting beliefs about yourself and the world to that invisible coat of yours.

Your task now then? Now that you know this, it is time to start taking off one layer at a time to discover more of who you really are.

I love the question my instructor shared from an EFT video while I was training to obtain my Certificate II in EFT: "If you could start again and do your life over, what part/s would you leave out? Which experiences would you delete and have not happen at all?" The event or events that first pop into your mind are usually the source of your most painful trauma or experiences. And therefore, are likely to be the thing/s that needs to be released and healed most.

There may be one, there may be many. Whatever the case may be for you, write them down and do all that you can to let go and begin your healing. Knowing that once you accept these experiences for what they are, not only will you be able to heal through forgiveness and release—you will soon see experiences with new eyes, new understanding and compassion for both yourself and others. That is, should you choose to allow for this in your reality.

What else can you do if you are ready to explore more of who you really are? There are no rules, no one-size-fits-all treatment. You simply need to start with one thing and if it feels right, keep doing it. If not, try something new.

Follow Your Intuition

Throughout my own personal development journey, there have been many different things I have tried and loved—and others I thought weren't helpful at all. Some things, I simply tried because they sounded like good ideas at the time. Some of the simplest sounding things, like the "secret letter burn exercise" from Chapter 3, clearing my head by being in nature, spending time with like-minded people and spiritual healers, meditation, yoga and journal writing have been very beneficial for me.

But just because these things work for me, may not mean they will work for you. You have to try things for yourself and see what happens. You will know if it works for you, because it will feel right or it won't. This is also a great way to practice strengthening your intuition, your own inner knowing.

Just start by exploring. What do other people around you do? What works for them? Is it something that resonates with you? Is it worth your time to give it a try?

We all connect with source, the divine, flow state in different ways. Let's look at someone like Gary Vanderchuk, founder of Vander Media, for example. Here's a guy that openly admits he has never meditated. In fact, he believes his ability to "hustle" and work ridiculously long hours, rarely losing energy or getting sick, is *his* gift. However, he knows that everyone is not built this way. Instead, he encourages others to become self-aware, as he knows that understanding yourself and how *you* tick is the best way to make the most of your life.

Writer and spiritual teacher, Denise Linn, encourages us to get out and be with nature, to connect and deepen our intuition. Best-selling author, speaker and spiritual teacher, Gabrielle Bernstein, speaks about how free writing and Kundalini meditation works for her and many others. Former professional League football player, author and entrepreneur, Lewis Howes, connects when playing sport, exercising, interviewing others on his podcast show and even while traveling on the train. Others find it through yoga, mindfulness, playing music, drawing, writing, gardening, cleaning or making art, to name a few.

The point of all these examples? They are simply there to show that there aren't any hard and fast rules. Everyone connects to all that is, to discover more of who they really are in their own way, and in the reality that works for them. What works for one may not work for another, so if you are finding it too darn hard to meditate, get out and go for a walk. Spend some time in nature, bring a notebook and pen (or not), and try that for a while. By giving something a go, you will soon discover what works for you.

When it comes to exploring, we just need to do it in a way that suits us, but most importantly, allows us enough time. Whether you call yourself spiritual or not, this doesn't need to be some "woo-woo" thing only hippies and monks do. This is simply about connecting to one's self. It is an act of self-love.

Loving who we are can be one of the most challenging tasks we will face. We often think we love ourselves but we have the "buts". "I love myself but I feel guilty for this, or bad for that." "I am not good enough." "I don't deserve love." "I don't deserve anything good." These are all things we learn over time from our parents, our family, our life, our society. These are the added layers that make our invisible coats so bulky in the first place.

We all want to be loved. We all want to give love. But hard times, sadness, painful memories, regret, shame and guilt create barriers. These are walls that we must break down, if and when we are ready. For if we don't do it now, if we don't learn the lessons we are here to learn, we must start over again. In this life or the next.

Authenticity

Becoming self-aware not only allows you to be authentically you, but it allows you to embrace love. When you know yourself, you won't want to be anyone but who you are. That's why people like Oprah, Marie Forleo, Adele, Carrie Green, Tony Robbins, Jim Rohn, Gary Vanderchuk, Kerwin Rae and Dr Wayne Dyer (I could go on for pages) are held in such high esteem. What we respect and connect with about these people is that even if they aren't your cup of tea, they are exactly themselves. They are authentic. They know what they are about and why they do what they do. They are extremely self-aware but also constantly learning and evolving. And when you see this in them—their authenticity, their realness—the trait that you see (in them or other people you resonate with) reflects your authenticity.

This message of getting to know who you really are by becoming more self-aware, is much of what this book is about. The truth of your reality comes from knowing who you are through self-awareness. Your reality is based on how you see yourself and the world. What you attract into your life reflects that. It mirrors every aspect of you. Therefore, the more self-aware you become, the more discerning you become, the more you can let go and the more you can be who you came here to be in this lifetime.

You are an amazing creature. And the fact that you are on this planet at this place and time, is not only a miracle, but no accident either. In fact, in a Ted Talk entitled, "Stop saying you are fine", criminal lawyer and one of the top career and relationship experts in America, Mel Robbins, talks about a study. In it, scientists calculated that the odds of any one of us being born at the exact time and space we were, to the parents we were born to, with the DNA structure we have and at the time we landed on this planet, is one in four trillion.

One in four trillion! Crikey!

That is no mean feat. With that in mind, you owe it to yourself and perhaps the betterment of the planet to start exploring you. To start stripping off those layers that are no longer serving you, to be all that you can be. All that you already are!

And the good news is, you don't need to do it all in one go. You can't anyway. What would be the point? You are here to learn lessons, evolve and grow, after all.

Check Point

- When looking back at your life, which experiences would you prefer to delete?

- What one thing can you do right now to bring you one step closer to healing? This may be a simple as booking in to talk to someone, performing the secret letter burn exercise, journaling, going for a walk or confiding in a trusted friend—whatever feels right for you.

Chapter 10

GAME ON

———————————

You are the creator of your own reality, the artist who not only holds the brush but is also the canvas. Whilst you may be here to learn specific lessons in this lifetime, the way you play the game of your life is completely up to you.

Your journey is just that. As Princess Leia says to Luke Skywalker in *Star Wars: A New Hope,* upon Han Solo's decision to not fly for the rebellion, "He's got to follow his own path. No one can choose it for him." And that is true for us all. We are the main character of our own "Choose Your Own Adventure" series. We get to make our reality whatever we choose. We play the game however we want to play it.

If planet Earth is the school, we are the students. Some of us will take to it like ducks to water, while others will find it one of the hardest things they ever do. All of us have our turn to be all that is before we can graduate into the next level—the next level of consciousness perhaps. And perhaps at different times. Eventually though, we all pass. All our lessons learned, our teaching done.

Whatever you want to believe is your choice. Your beliefs, always present in your life, reflecting what you believe to be true. It really is that simple. You are the one who puts meaning into all that is when it comes to your reality. There is no right or wrong. It just is. You decide. You create. You make it happen.

Want to believe that life is a struggle, everything is terrible and you will never have enough? That is what you are likely to get. Want to believe that there are great people out there and that miracles happen every day? Then that is what you are likely to get. You will interpret things your way. It is your birthright. It is part of the human experience. You get to choose. No one else can make that decision for you—unless you let them. Again, that's your choice. It is your reality after all.

So, What Next?

If the idea of being more of who you are excites, challenges and interests you, you have already answered yes to the first question and that is, are you willing to explore?

With that in mind, as you put on your Explorer's t-shirt and begin to question the truth of your reality, it is key for you to remember this next important step. It's one we have yet to touch on throughout the book, but one I believe is essential.

As you begin to take off the layers of your invisible coat and become more of you, wherever you can, you must always remember to have fun along the way. You know, belly laugh until you nearly pee your pants. Learn to laugh at yourself. Dance like no one is watching. Sing to your favourite song at the top of your lungs, whether you can hold a note or not. Love with all that you have, and give to yourself with all that you've got.

At the end day, there are so many options in the world, and all you can do is explore, seek, discover and grow. Follow your intuition. If something doesn't feel right, it usually isn't. Don't question it, follow your inner guidance, your gut, your knowingness. Remember your connection to it all. Remembering that anything positive you do for yourself has a massive effect, not just for you, but for everyone. Geez, you are amazing. Magnificent, in fact!

And the best part? Every day, you get to choose how you are going to be, what you are going to do and how you are going to do it. By setting your intentions, by choosing thoughts that lift you up, by working through the tough days (because we are human after all), by creating feelings as if you already have what it is you desire, by believing in yourself and by taking action, even if just one tiny step each day, you are creating your own reality in each and every moment.

Not only that, as you travel this road of self-growth, understanding and self-awareness, you will become more and more aware of the power and magnificence of you. You will learn to forgive both yourself and others. You will accept what is, let go and move forward—or simply be willing to if you're not yet ready, in order to heal.

You will respect and value who you are and the importance of your role in being *you*, your unique, amazing self on this planet. Then through it all, you will begin to love yourself more and more each day. And with that, you will provide not only yourself but the entire universe, with the greatest gift of all: unconditional love.

AFTERWORD

If you have read this far, I would like to thank you for being with me through the pages of this book. When I started writing and re-writing this book, I was slowly but surely taking off another layer of my own invisible coat, the layer of the coat that keeps so many of us stuck: the caring-too-much-what-everyone-thinks layer. This layer is one that I have worn for many years—and, in fairness to myself, I have loosened it quite a bit over time. However, like you, I am human, and putting myself, my thoughts and my take on the world in the form of a book is scary, exhilarating, exciting and challenging all in one.

But I can't *not* do it. I am ready to be all that I am. To let my light shine in the unique way that it was designed to shine. I know that not everyone will resonate with what I am here to offer, and that is okay. We don't all like the same music, nor do we have the same favourite foods, after all. And as I have said from the beginning, I am not here to tell you what music or food to like anyway.

All I want, if I could flick a switch and have it be done, is for each of us to remember just how powerful we are. That it doesn't matter who you were yesterday. What matters is who you choose to be today, that we are the creators of our own reality. Magnificent creatures who, when we become self-aware and learn to follow our own intuition and guidance, remember that at the core of it all, are all here to be exactly who we are. To let our light shine as bright as it can shine and to be love. In turn, this will create a ripple effect and empower others to do just the same. Because really, the person you are and who you will always be is perfect. And there ain't no one else in this entire universe who can be a better version of you than you.

That is what I really want.

That, and world peace. Nothing too crazy.

ACKNOWLEDGMENTS

From the bottom of my heart, I would like to thank everyone who has ever been part of my life in any way. I have created this reality in which I now live, and have lived up until this moment, and without each experience I would not be where I am today. For that, I am truly grateful.

To my amazing man, Simon, thank you for being all that you are. To my beautiful family, dear friends, editors and those who have been a part of my email list and social networks past, present, future—thank you for allowing me to share my thoughts with you every week. I know you already know this, but it is such a gift and honour to be able to do this. I have loved every comment you have ever shared and appreciate the continued support and encouragement you give me. Thank you, thank you, thank you.

And to you (yes, you!) reading this right now. Thank you for being you and for being willing to embrace the exploration and the experience of simply being human. Put simply, you rock!

RESOURCES

Online

The Art of Manifesting live talk by Dr Wayne Dyer, Wanderlust Event, 2012
www.wanderlust.com/journal/wayne-dyer-master-art-manifesting

How to stop screwing yourself over by Mel Robbins, TEDxSF
www.youtube.com/watch?v=Lp7E973zozc

Gregg Braden
www.greggbraden.com

Gregg Braden explains the 7 Essence Mirrors
www.youtube.com/watch?v=rcFCgJmIFow

Gregg Braden talks about the Gospel of Thomas
www.youtube.com/watch?v=y4dPzfKwQVM

Gregg Braden on the Dead Sea Scrolls
www.youtube.com/watch?v=1JMELyhuvws

Gregg Braden talks showing the tumour disappearing in medicine-less hospital in China
www.youtube.com/watch?v=I2ohSOzV4SQ&t=2s
www.youtube.com/watch?v=4pGYPyiE4ng

Cancer Healing in China posted by LiveRockMusic2010
www.youtube.com/watch?v=HecA7XRO7eQ

Note: Due to the fluid nature of the Internet, some resources listed may change or become unavailable, however were correct at the time of publishing.

Books

Dying to be Me by Anita Moorgani

Overcoming Multiple Sclerosis by George Jelenik
www.overcomingms.org

Proof of Heaven by Dr Eben Alexander

Think and Grow Rich by Napoleon Hill – The Original 1937 Unedited Edition
www.naphill.org

References from *Think and Grow Rich* by Napoleon Hill – The Original 1937 Unedited Edition

RESOURCES

"THOUGHTS WHICH ARE MIXED WITH ANY OF THE FEELINGS OF EMOTIONS, CONSTITUTE A "MAGNETIC" FORCE WHICH ATTRACTS, FROM THE VIBRATIONS OF THE ETHER, OTHER SIMILAR, OR RELATED THOUGHTS."

Page 72, 1937 Unedited Edition
Page 26, Kindle Edition

"The ether in which this little earth floats, in which we move and have our being, is a form of energy moving at an inconceivably high rate of vibration, and that the ether is filled with a form of universal power which ADAPTS itself to the nature of the thoughts we hold in our minds; and INFLUENCES us, in natural ways, to transmute our thoughts into their physical equivalent."

Page 32, 1937 Unedited Edition
Page 8, Kindle Edition

"The ether is a great cosmic mass of eternal forces of vibration. It is made up of both destructive vibrations and constructive vibrations. It carries, at all times, vibrations of fear, poverty, disease, failure, misery; and vibrations of prosperity, health, success, and happiness, just as surely as it carries the sound of hundreds of orchestrations of music, and hundreds of human voices, all of which maintain their own individuality, and means of identification, through the medium of radio."

Page 72, 1937 Unedited Edition
Page 26, Kindle Edition

ABOUT THE AUTHOR

Nereeda McInnes is a writer, business and marketing mentor, certified life-coach and Founder of nereedamcinnes.com. She is also trained in various healing modalities and is a passionate advocate for personal development, growth and exploring all that we are on a deeper level. Working with people from all walks of business and life to cultivate belief and create a reality that is in line with what it is people truly want, as opposed to what they think they 'should', Nereeda speaks, writes and inspires others to play the game of life their way.

MORE FROM THE AUTHOR

You can find more from the author at the following places:

Website
www.nereedamcinnes.com

Facebook
www.facebook.com/NereedaMcInnes/

Instagram
www.instagram.com/nereedamcinnes/

LinkedIn
www.linkedin.com/in/nereedamcinnes

Twitter
www.twitter.com/nereedamcinnes

CPSIA information can be obtained
at www.ICGtesting.com
Printed in the USA
BVHW091121181021
619205BV00015B/530